GRANDFATHER,

Tell Me Again How We Are All Related

red feather smooth stone press

Grandfather, Tell Me Again How We Are All Related. Text copyright © 2024 by Delena Rose.

redfeathersmoothstone@gmail.com
www.redfeathersmoothstone.com

ISBN: 978-1-0691895-0-9

For my son, Skye Dancing Hawk

The boy left his cabin and headed
down the narrow path into the
deep woods. He came here often
and did not have to go very far.

The moss was soft and springy
under his feet as he silently made
his way toward his favourite
resting spot.

A thick root, flat and curled like a
seat, invited him to come and sit,
and even stay a while.

It was quiet in the deep woods. The
air was cool and fresh. The boy's
grandfather was already there,
waiting patiently for him.

In the distance, a raven cawed—and
then it stopped. Everything became
still and peaceful. It was the perfect
moment to ask his favourite
question.

"Grandfather," the boy began, his
voice soft, "tell me again how we are
all related."

As always, there was a long pause.
The grandfather smiled, and
when he finally spoke, his voice
was deep and calm, like the sound
of steady wind blowing through
the treetops.

"Yes, Grandchild, I will tell you
again how we are all related, for
this story can never be told too
many times."

The boy settled deeper into the
roots of the tree, one small hand
resting on the rough bark. As he
quieted himself, he could sense
the comforting pulse of life under
his fingertips.

"Do you see the spider," his grandfather began, "spinning her web between the branches?" The boy looked at the delicate spider busily weaving her web nearby. Her long legs moved skillfully across each silken thread.

"See how her legs reach out in eight directions, forming a circle. From branch to branch and leaf to leaf, she spins and weaves her web... Look, another circle. Each strand intentionally placed, each strand an important part of her creation.

"A skilled weaver of the web, the spider teaches us that everything, both seen and unseen, is connected in the sacred web of life.

We are all related."

"And look, there," the grandfather continued, "hidden in the grass." The boy smiled at the tiny mouse scurrying softly on the ground. Her movements were quick and efficient as she busily gathered bits of leaves to warm her nest.

"Unlike the hawk who soars high above and sees the world from a distance, the mouse remains on the ground, kissing the earth with every tiny paw print. She explores her world up close, touching and sniffing, and carefully noticing every detail around her.

"A quick and keen observer, the mouse teaches us to touch the earth with reverence, and to pay attention to the details of life.

We are all related."

Just then, a squirrel appeared. A fearless acrobat high in the trees, it playfully leapt from branch to branch. The boy and his grandfather laughed at its lively dance through the woods. "The squirrel reminds us that we, too, need to stretch our legs, to run freely, and to play."

Now on the ground, the squirrel held a hazelnut in its nimble paws. The grandfather continued, "The squirrel understands the seasons of life, knowing that the abundance of summer and autumn is always followed by winter's scarcity.

"As a forager and gatherer, the squirrel teaches us to enjoy life while also being prepared for change.

We are all related."

As the boy continued to sit quietly, he sensed a small movement nearby. Looking around, he finally spotted the rabbit, now sitting perfectly still. Her soft, brown fur blended seamlessly with the low brush so that she almost seemed to disappear from view.

As the rabbit began to nibble on some grass, the boy admired her long, velvety ears and powerful hind legs. His grandfather explained, "The rabbit listens intently, paying attention to small sounds that others may miss. Her strong hind legs allow her to move with lightening speed when faced with danger.

"Gentle and calm, yet nimble and fast, the rabbit reminds us to cherish every moment of life.

We are all related."

"Now," whispered the grandfather,
"here comes the fox."

The boy watched as the slender
red fox moved silently in the
shadows nearby. As she hunted,
her sharp ears listened for every
sound, instincts keen and alert.
She sniffed the ground, poking her
narrow nose into every nook and
cranny.

She suddenly paused, becoming
very still... then leapt high into the
air, her sleek body arching
gracefully as she dove toward a
small, empty burrow.

"Following the golden threads of
her curiosity, the fox teaches us
that there is wisdom to be found
in every wild place.

We are all related."

Not long after, a coyote ran past. He was limping and seemed to be in a hurry. In his haste, he tripped over a tree root and rolled a few times, stirring up a cloud of dust. Springing back up, he shook his fur vigorously and glanced back at the boy to see if he was watching.

The boy *was* watching. The coyote smiled, his eyes playful and mischievous. "Did he do that on purpose?" the boy asked his grandfather. His grandfather laughed and replied, "This adaptable and cunning joker with his clever wild ways, reminds us that not all paths are straight, but that some twist and turn and lead us to unexpected places.

"As trickster and teacher, coyote reminds us to laugh while looking for the lessons in every experience—especially the challenging ones.

We are all related."

The boy got up to stretch his legs. From this new position, he caught a fleeting glimpse of a large grey wolf. She was standing perfectly still, watching him curiously from a distance. Then, in an instant, she turned and disappeared. "It is a rare thing to see a wolf in the wild," the grandfather said. "Except when raising young, they are always on the move.

"Wolves hunt and roam as a family, living together in harmony. Each member has a role to play and each member's gifts and strengths are honoured and valued. The wolf understands that her greatest strength is not as an individual, but in being a part of the pack.

"As wise leaders, wolves teach us that true alpha males and females are not necessarily the strongest, but the ones who are best able to maintain harmony within the pack.

We are all related."

From a distance, the boy spotted a bear. She was busy eating berries, pulling the branches toward her and eating the fruit right off of the branches. The grandfather explained, "The bear feasts throughout the summer and fall, storing up body fat so that she can rest and dream throughout the long, dark winter.

"She walks the sacred path of the healer, carrying the knowledge of medicine plants. Awakening in the spring, she digs up bitter herbs and roots to cleanse and nourish her body.

"As a medicine keeper, the bear teaches us to listen to our body's need for deep rest, and to learn which plants heal us and keep us strong.

We are all related."

As the day was coming to a close, one final visitor—a barred owl, made her ghostly appearance. Flying overhead, she moved through the air on silent wings and landed on a branch nearby.

The grandfather smiled at his familiar friend and said, "The owl watches silently, her wide eyes peering through the darkest of night. Observing all the creatures in the woods, both large and very small, she sees the patterns and cycles of life. Recognizing the divine order beneath the chaos, she understands that all of life is connected and in relationship with one another.

"As one-who-sees-in-the-dark, the owl reminds us to listen to our inner wisdom and to trust that there is purpose and meaning to everything in life.

We are all related."

"And now," the grandfather's voice grew soft. "Let us speak of *you*. Just as the spider spins her web and the owl sees every part of it, you, too, have a place in this world. Your laughter, your love, even your quiet thoughts are all threads in the sacred web of life."

The boy felt his heart fill with wonder. "So, I, too, am a part of the web?" he asked, his voice barely above a whisper. "Yes," the grandfather smiled. "You are connected to every creature, every stone, and every tree.

"As a child of this earth, you teach us all to see the world anew, and that respect for all our relations holds our world together in a good way.

We are all related."

"Thank you, Grandfather," the boy
whispered, his small voice carrying up
through the branches.

His grandfather laughed softly, his
voice warm and full of love. "I am
always here, little one, for I am the
grandfather of all things. My roots
hold the soil and my branches frame
the sky. When you sit with me, you sit
with all that is."

The boy's eyes widened as he looked up at the great tree, understanding at last, the source of this quiet, familiar voice.

The tree was his grandfather—the voice that had always guided him, teaching him to value every creature, from the smallest spider to the mightiest bear.

The boy wrapped his arms around his grandfather, sensing the ancient heartbeat and becoming one with the great tree.

He realized that he finally understood, from the deepest part of himself, the teaching that is true for all of us— that we are *all* connected to *everything*.

We are all related.

About the Author

A Metis, born in the Pas, Manitoba, Delena was raised between Winnipeg and Cormorant, Manitoba. She is the eldest child of Barb Nabess and Don Jashyn (Ukrainian heritage) and grandchild to John and Rose Nabess. Currently, she resides in Treaty Six Territory in central Alberta and is registered with the Metis Nation of Alberta,

Delena holds a Bachelor of Science (majoring in Biology with a minor in Art & Design), Bachelor of Education, and Master of Education in Indigenous Peoples Education from the University of Alberta. Her graduate thesis received an award from the Canadian Association for Teacher Education. Throughout her career, she primarily worked with Indigenous communities across Alberta, either as an educator, writer, or program manager in collaboration with the federal and provincial governments.

In 2011, Delena moved "back to the bush" where she lives with her family in a cabin on Pigeon Lake, Alberta. She lives a magical life in the woods and is visited regularly by the insects, birds and animals featured in her stories. When Delena is not writing or homeschooling her son, she spends her time gardening, tending to her goats and chickens, giving plant medicine workshops, leading drum circles, selling her handmade jewelry at local markets, and serving her community as an Animator with the Rural Mental Health Project (Canadian Mental Health Association).

A grandfather teaches his grandson how we are all related to plants, insects, birds, and animals—and that each of us has a place in the sacred web of life.

red feather
smooth stone
press

www.redfeathersmoothstone.com

ISBN 978-1-0691895-0-9

A grandfather teaches his grandson how we are all
related to plants, insects, birds, and animals—and that
each of us has a place in the sacred web of life.

red feather
smooth stone
press

www.redfeathersmoothstone.com

ISBN 978-1-0691895-0-9
61699
9 781069 189509

Sweet
River's Recipes
By: Shaneka & River Demps